OIL FOR LIFE

Miriam Whitehead-Brice

BROAD WING PRESS
CAPITAL HEIGHTS, MD

Copyright © 2020 Miriam Whitehead-Brice

All rights reserved. No parts of this book may be reproduced in any form without written permission from Broad Wing Publications.

Unless otherwise noted, Scripture is taken from the Holy Bible, New King James Version®. Copyright© 1982 by Thomas Nelson, Inc. Used by permission. All rights reserved.

Printed in the United States of America

ISBN: 13: 978-1-938373-48-0

*"Let your garments always be white,
And let your head lack no oil"
(Ecclesiastes 9:8).*

Table of Contents

Dear Courage	1
Forget The Regrets	2
I've Fallen Short	3
Change Me First	4
I Think Myself…	5
Why Worry	6
You're Not Alone	7
Accepting No	8
Forgiveness	9
Quality / Quantity	10
Source / Resource	11
Confidence	12
The Place of Time	13
Opponents/Footstools	14
Profits / Prophets	15
Intentional Noise	16
Testimonies	17
God Says	18
Jesus Flipped the Script	19
Pat On The Back	20
He's The Difference	21
People	22
You're Equipped	23
Let It Go	24
He Woke You	25
Move Forward	26
He Looks Out	27

While You Were	28
Emotional/Intentional	29
100% Looks Like	30
Distractions	31
Yet Will I Trust	32
Whole Healed Go	33
Power and	34
Baggage	35
The Oil	36
P.U.S.H.	37
Broken Is Okay	38
It's For Him	39
Rejection	40
The Yoke	41
Freedom With	42
Anyhow	43
Know Who's On	44
S. E. R. V. E.	45
I'm A Prisoner	46
Fearful Or Faithful	47
Last To First	48
More Than You Can	49
Through	50
Disabled	51
Called and Chosen	52
Addiction/Deliverance	53
Intensify	54
The Others	55

Man	56
God	57
Rise Above To Win	58
The Lord Changeth Not	59
Why	60
Search Me	61
It's In Your Hands	62
I Receive It	63
Give	64
Fall Back	65

Dear Courage

I have embraced trauma unwillingly. I have kissed my version of death. I've felt like I was at the end of my rope, and I've always blamed myself. I thought that certain things were behind me, but memories don't easily fade. I have fondled the hardcore notion that my strength has been weakened by my mental disfigurement. I'd become my own worst enemy.

Facing failures should not hinder me. Fear should not resemble me. Someone needs me more than I need to hide. This is where faith and you, my "Courage," collide.

"Be of good courage, and let us be strong for our people and for the cities of our God. And may the LORD do what is good in His sight." **(2 Samuel 10:12)**

Forget the Regrets

I must forget my regrets, or I will not move past my now. I can't change yesterday, so I'll accept what God allowed. It is for my good and no other reason and concentrating on those things will drive me crazy. "Shake it off," I tell myself. The past was a test to challenge and ensure my best.

I can't change yesterday. I can accept that yesterday has changed me. Jesus knows what I've been through, and only he knows what I'll go through. He's been my covering since then, as He's covering me now. Since the Lord has forgiven my past, I will concentrate on "Forward." I will not hold onto the regrets. I will just bask in gratefulness. The Lord made a way somehow.

"For You formed my inward parts; You covered me in my mother's womb." **(Psalm 139:13)**

I've Fallen Short

I have fallen short. I've messed up, Lord. My will and yours weren't on one accord. Forgive me, father!

I receive my forgiveness with love. There's no condemning cloud lingering above my head. My reprimand comes with security. There is still liberty in my journey. What I've gone through does not disturb my purpose. It finesses my existence for His glory. My shortcomings are His uprisings. When I am weak, He is made strong. My valley lows are actually my mountain songs. Thank you, Jesus, as I continue on!

"I find then a law, that evil is present with me, the one who wills to do good." **(Romans 7:21)**

Change Me First

I must admit that I have been complaining about others and their actions, but mines are not exempt. Lord, as you change them, change, me. I am your child, and my will chases after thee. As you induce in others the will for them to change, I will repent and learn to accept their change.

Change my attitude in the workplace so they will see your light in me. Change my heart for my community. Adjust my thoughts for the sake of my family. Let the Christ in me be revealed. Change this clay into what you may. This wound needs spiritual healing.

"For our citizenship is in heaven, from which we also eagerly wait for the Savior, the Lord Jesus Christ, who will transform our lowly body that it may be conformed to His glorious body, according to the working by which He's able even to subdue all things to Himself." **(Philippians 3:20)**

I Think Myself Happy

When I try to live through another's happiness, my loneliness becomes evident. I think of what the Lord has done for me, and joy steps forward and smiles with presence. I think myself happy and pray for the sad around me. I will not depend on loved ones, friends, and others to make me happy. Come what may, I think myself happy when bad news challenges my position. I think myself happy and persevere with assurance.

I think myself happy and operate in love. I think myself happy because He loved me first, and His love is constant and unconditional. I think myself happy even when life's trials bend to propose. I think myself happy as I dwell happily in the Lord. "

I think myself happy, King Agrippa, because today I shall answer for myself ... " **(Act 26:2)**

Why Worry

We have heard and said this saying, "If you're going to worry, don't pray, and if you're going to pray, don't worry." Faith is a marvelous thing when applied daily. Smile and just walk on.

We rely on technology, machines, people, pills, and (horoscopes-stop it), without a second thought. For some reason depending on the Lord requires a knee bending, oil anointing, 5-fold ministry, prayer-line advocacy, shut-in ministry process, when all you have to do, is ask! Fasting and praying are requirements for some things! In your walk with Jesus daily, also trust in him fervently. Let the "Nay-Sayers" worry.

"Therefore do not worry about tomorrow, for tomorrow will worry about its own things. Sufficient for the day is its own trouble." **(Matthew 6:34)**

You're Not Alone

You are not alone; you are set apart. Some people are in your life that cannot go where you are going. Like a rocket is being sent up, pieces are designed to drop off because they're not built for the height and distance for which the rocket is destined.

You aren't aware of the "Doubting Thomas" in your clique. Some people just aren't for you. Some of us refuse to let go of people and things. Some of us tell everything to those we think are for us; then wonder why we can't go any further than where we are.

At times we go through unnecessary situations because of who we are connected to. Enjoy being set apart. Relax in your time alone with Jesus. Listen and enjoy.

***"But know that the LORD has set apart for Himself him who is godly…"* (Psalm 4:3)**

Accepting No

When the answer is, "No," it's not the end of the world! Since the Lord holds yesterday, today, and forevermore, His decisions are best. Whether you accept it or not, the Lord does not have to give a reason about why things are. Just understand that He knows what is best. Whether it is concerning a lost loved one, a relationship, a dream, a want, or a need. His will is not emotional; it's intentional.

At times we can't see beyond a right now circumstance. Trust in the Lord! The Lord sees beyond. The Lord sees beyond. He dwells in always!

"Trust in the LORD with all your heart and lean not on your own understanding; In all your ways acknowledge Him, And He shall direct your paths." **(Proverbs 3:5-6)**

Forgiveness

Forgiveness embraces love and freedom.

Forgive those who have knowingly hurt you. Forgive those who seek to despitefully use you. Forgive those who have sought to destroy you.

How long must you dwell in that stagnant place called hurt? How long will you let unforgiving emotions rule over you? How long will you let unforgiving attitudes dictate your relationships? How long will you let bitterness and resentment corner you into low self-esteem?

Ask for forgiveness for being unforgiving. Forgiveness destroys yokes. Forgiveness condemns bondage. Asking for forgiveness can break the chains of pride. Jesus forgave us!

"Lord, how often shall my brother sin against me, and I forgive him?... Jesus said to him, "I do not say to you, up to seven times, but up to seventy times seven."
(Matthew 18:21, 22)

Quality vs. Quantity

In a lot of instances, the world represents "quantity." How high is your credits score? How many reward points or how much money do you have? What is your credit card limit? Bar codes are on everything!

Jesus represents "Quality." Faith has placed believers in homes, positions, and in financial standings with low credit scores, no reward points, no qualifications, and with bad backgrounds. It's nice to have good credit, credit cards, and reward points. Just know that if you don't, Jesus works great in these situations. Watch him show up and shut down any phrase, mindset, or action that says, "You can't and you won't." Watch those words and thoughts turn to "how, when, and wow!

"And everyone who has this hope in Him purifies himself, just as He is pure." **(1 John 3:3)**

Source and Resource

The prefix "re" means to repeat. The world is full of resources. Jesus has provided people with gifts and talents to help his people, who also have gifts and talents. No one person is everything. He has given Doctors talents for the human body. He has given Psychiatrist listening skills, blue-collar and white-collar gifts, and talents, and so on. These are Resources that you'll go back and use repeatedly.

Jesus is a one-time Source. The Father, Son, and Holy Ghost; is the mind, body, and spirit all wrapped up in one. If there is a need for a "re" of anything, it's for the body and mind. Believe wholly in the true living Source.

"And my God shall supply all your need according to His riches in glory by Christ Jesus." **(Philippians 4:19)**

Confidence

Get past yourself, your doubts, trust issues, low self-esteem, and all of your idiosyncrasies. Then that mirrored reflection can't be told something negative. You are your worst enemy. That Helmet of Salvation is important, and when applied properly it can withstand even self-induced issues. You can pick your own self up.

Others' opinions and validations won't be necessary when you know that you know whose you are. When you put on the whole armor of God, make sure you use it properly. The darts of the enemy will bounce off. Nothing can penetrate; nothing can breakthrough, saturate, or invade the property of God.

Come up out of that grave. Shake off those rags of fear, doubt, confusion, and uncertainty. You've been washed in the blood of the Lamb. LOOK! SEE!

*"And take the helmet of salvation..." (***Ephesians 6:17)**

The Place Of Time

While there's nothing new under the sun, things have an order to them. The sun and the moon have an order. Times of birth for all creatures have an occasion. Yes, everything has its purpose. Occupy your time to the fullest.

Time was invested in you. Jesus' birth, life, death, and resurrection took time. His sacrifice was for you. He has placed time in you. So you have a time to rise and a time to sit. There's a time to mourn and a time to make a joyous noise; a time to fast and pray; a time to praise and worship him; and a time to minister to others. There's a time to exist and a time to die. What are you doing with your time? While there's still time!

"To everything there is a season, and a time to every purpose under the heaven." **(Ecclesiastes 3:1)**

Footstools

We wrestle not against flesh and blood. So, those who always allow the enemy to use them as devices to do you harm in any way are called, footstools. Since victory is already the Lord's, and you are a "Child of The King;" please note that everything the enemy meant to harm you with is just a stacking stool that you will stand on.

On this platform, you will be able to testify of how the Lord brought you through. Let it grow higher and higher as you reach new levels in Christ. So stand tall upon the enemy and watch as the Lord prepares a table in front of them.

"...Thou preparest a table before me in the presence of mine enemies..." **(Psalm 23:5)**

Profits / Prophets

Beware of the soothsayers, astrologists, mind readers, palm readers, and false teachers. Read your Bible and tune in to what you're reading. Accountability also lies with you. Don't base your freedom on others. They cannot qualify you for Christ. You are responsible for your eternal life. Following the crowd is a bad decision.

These twenty-first century Pharisees and Sadducees seek an earthly gain. Their reward exists right here. Some leaders say they're for Christ and ignore answerability and the anointing has been taken. It's sad to think that they're still behind pulpits. They'll answer to the Maker, as we all will. Beware! Be aware!

"But I say to you that for every idle word men may speak, they will give account of it in the day of judgment." **(Matthew 12:36)**

Intentional Noise

It is imperative that we pay attention to what we allow through our gates. *"Lift up your heads, O ye gates; and be ye lift up, ye everlasting doors; and the King of glory shall come in."* **(Psalm 24:7).** This also applies to the kinds of music you listen to. Satan was the prince of the air before being thrown from Heaven. He uses music, lyrics, arguments, gossiping, and different noises to distract you. Sometimes your mind gets muddled, because of the things you hear.

David's ability to play the harp was Godly, strategic, and intentional. What kind of noise are you making? Pay attention to what you're listening to, because your spirit does!

"Make a joyful noise unto the Lord..." **(Psalm 100:1)**

Testimonies

Speaking of where God has brought you from is a freeing experience. It's to help another, so they'll see the possibilities of deliverance. Do you think He just did it for you?

It's okay to know that the Saints of God had a past. Too often people forget where they've come from and see where others are and get mad, whisper, gossip, and judge!

We were all born in sin, but our past has been forgiven. Tell of the goodness of Jesus. Speak of how he's kept you when you were in your mess. It's okay to recall the horrible days that lay in yesterday's place. Where you are now is a blessing. You've been restored through the Lord's righteousness. Testify!

"And they overcame him by the blood of the Lamb and by the word of their testimony, and they did not love their lives to the death." **(Revelation 12:11)**

God Says

   hen others attempt to downgrade you, with confidence, you declare that you have purpose. God says, **"...we are his people, and the sheep of his pasture..." (Psalm 100:3)** We are His sheep and He is our Shepherd. So, listen up wolves, you've been rebuked go back from whence you came.

   God says *"...we are more than conquerors...."* **(Romans 8:37)** That means the battle is already won. So, you're walking with your head held high into a victory that's already done. God says, *"I can do all things through Christ which strengtheneth me." (*Philippians **4:13)** Let your faith override your doubt. Let your confidence overwhelm your fears. Your security outlines your destiny. Your yesterdays are in the rear.

"...I am fearfully and wonderfully made: ..." (Psalm 139:14)

Jesus Flipped The Script

"The thief cometh not, but for to steal, and to kill, and to destroy…" **(John 10:10)** The enemy has no good intentions when it comes to you. Don't get distracted by the obstacles in this world. The enemy robbed you of your happiness and deprived you of peace. The enemy seeks to destroy purpose. He gets personal!

Let Jesus take away your anger. Give Him your frustrations. He will resuscitate your gladness and overthrow your sadness with happiness. Just fall into the will of Jesus. He's waiting with his arms open wide. Restoration is yours. Recovering those things that are yours is not a distant dream. You are meant to live in abundance!

"… I am come that they might have life, and that they might have it more abundantly." **(John 10:10)**

A Pat On The Back

What kind of person are you? Do you need to be encouraged always; even to wave your hand? Is life being a drag to you? Are you motivated to do things whether or not there is something in return? What is your reason for doing things? What is your agenda?

As you that look at me; do you look at what I've done; do you notice me as a person? Is "I" more important than "we?" I'm not saying ignore yourself, but is it always about you? Do you do just to receive? If you don't live in that perspective, disappointment won't be so severe.

Be that joyous person giving thanks in all that you do. Realize that being a prisoner of the Savior is a reward that the world can't give you. Your life expectancy is eternal!

"And whatever you do, do it heartily, as to the Lord and not to men." **(Colossians 3:23)**

He's The Difference

Jesus makes a difference in you. Man deems people crazy that can smile through devastation; that can still praise Him in the midst of a storm, and that can be grateful during life-changing events

With Christ on your side, who can come against you? With Christ within you, He can turn a cold heart into a warm and loving heart. The difference in your decisions is Jesus. The difference in your walk and talk is Jesus.

It may be strange to the world. They make money off of changing people. Your price was paid on the cross. Jesus made the difference between what you were and who you are now in Christ Jesus. When they ask why or how, tell them the difference is Jesus.

*"But you are a chosen generation, a royal priesthood, a holy nation, His own special people…" (***1 Peter 2:9**)

People

Dealing with mankind when they aren't so kind is difficult. Staying prayed up is necessary when dealing with people. People are going to be people, always. You have to communicate and associate with them. Yes, they come with issues. So do you, until Jesus, and then after Jesus! Being kindhearted to those who despitefully use, you can be a challenge. Tit-for-tat and revenge are practices that will control and consume you.

Be that person that says hello and good-bye. Be that person that listens and shows concern. Be that person who understands that every day isn't a sunny one to the world. Be that person that illuminates with the love of Jesus. Be and operate, as Jesus' people should.

"As the Father has loved me, so have I loved you: continue ye in my love." **(John 15:9)**

You're Equipped

What's inside of you? Fear isn't! In Christ, you have already been equipped with everything you need to stand on the battlefield and work in the Vineyard. Halleluiah! Battlefield requirements: "the whole armor of God..."—your loins girt about with truth, the breastplate of righteousness; preparation of the gospel of peace; the shield of faith, the helmet of salvation, and the sword of the Spirit. *(Ephesians 6:1--17)* Vineyard attributes: "Fruits of the Spirit"—love, joy, peace, longsuffering, gentleness, goodness, faith, meekness, and temperance. **(Galatians 5:22-23)**

If you don't know or understand the equipment, I urge you to pray, read the Bible, and watch the Lord perform the miraculous in your life. When putting a bike together, you read the manual or instruction book for it. You read the manual for putting together a shelf for the bike. Follow the instructions of the manual written by your Creator, the "Lord God Almighty." In faith, mountains will move. Trials will come; stand and you will be strengthened.

"Put on the whole armour of God..." **(Ephesians 6:13)**

Let It Go

Let go of those feelings of hatred that will keep you bound. Let go of those old friendships that are out of season, now. Release what you can't change and pray for the changes you can. Walk in the newness of God. Let go of that 'old man.' Let loose of that excess baggage. Eliminate those emotions that keep circling around you. Watch the dead weight come off and your walk will be easier. Feel your faith expand as you exist in freedom. Shake off that worry that blocks your trust. Pray or worry. Only one can come forth.

Embrace your slimming down. Enjoy your new size. Be joyful in that new creature that the mirror gives you, because of Christ.

"Therefore, if anyone is in Christ, he is a new creation; old things have passed away; behold, all things have become new." **(2 Corinthians 5:17)**

He Woke You

He woke you get up. It wasn't an alarm clock. A new day was given to you at 12:01 a.m. You slept on a pillow of goodness and mercy.

Since He woke you up, get up and move. This is another chance to get it right. Make amends and ask for forgiveness. Your sound mind was a gift that so many others did not receive today. Your existence was a gift so many others did not receive today. Jesus woke you up for a reason; for a purpose; and for a person. Someone is watching you and waiting for a cause to live, intent to press on, or an inspirational word from you.

You are a beacon of light for those in darkness. Someone is watching. They will ask "What must I do to be saved?"

"Therefore He says: Awake, you who sleep, Arise from the dead, And Christ will give you light." **(Ephesians 5:14)**

Move Forward

Knowing that your sins are forgiven should initiate thoughts of gratefulness. Living and dwelling in the past will keep you stagnant. Condemnation is not of God. Release those factions of yesterday. Let go of that anger. Don't hold on to those dangerous relationships that this new season doesn't call for. Their understanding of your divine purpose is limited.

You can't see where you're walking looking backward. Move forward. Don't second guess what the Lord has put in you. People are watching and thirsting for what you possess that is keeping you from where they are now. Move forward!

"Do not remember the sins of my youth, nor my transgressions; According to Your mercy remember me, For Your goodness' sake, O LORD." **(Psalms 25:7)**

He Looks Out

Jesus looks out for you; when the world tries to stammer your voice. He'll shut them down and make a space for you to speak. Those who mistreat you will answer to him. The Lord will cover you from the vultures. He will make you aware of the test and trials that only come to make you stronger for the next level in Him. Jesus will show up, to shut up, shut out, and shut down man's agenda, just for you. You are important to him. He loves you. He has great things in place, just for you!

Not only is Jesus looking out for you He is working things out for your behalf. He will meet you where you are. Just sink into the everlasting arms of Jesus and bask in the comforts of his will.

"No weapon formed against you shall prosper, And every tongue which rises against you in judgment You shall condemn." **(Isaiah 54:17)**

While You Were Asleep

While you were asleep, there was a battle going on. There was a fight for your stead. The Adversary was in the Lord's ear saying, "Look at your sheep; they can't get it together. Let me trouble their minds and their earthly matters. Immediately heavens angels were dispatched, and the wrestlers of principalities had met their match. While you tossed and turned without a care, God was waking you up to a new day that was already prepared. As you opened your eyes and greeted the sun, placing your feet on the floor meant another victory was won.

So, before you go to sleep pray! Tomorrow isn't promised although you've made plans to live there. What are you listening to before you sleep? Inspirational praises entertaining the air can bring down strongholds as you lay asleep.

***"The Lord shall fight for you…"* (Exodus 14:14)**

Emotional / Intentional

Happy, sad, confused, smiling, moody, secure, insecure, grateful, hateful, lonely, itchy, cranky, moody, distant, friendly, bothered, depressed, manic, tearful, joyful, unsure, playful, sure, doubtful, worrisome, boastful, angry, salty, envious, jealousy, caring, loving, mean, spiteful, ornery, cheerful, and grouchy. These emotions come and go. It's a people thing!

Faithful, trusting, authentic, powerful, keeper, provider, deliverer, truthful, perfect, constant, loyal, great, consistent, Holy, righteous, sovereign, comforter, healer, love, wonderful, keeper, marvelous, jealous, devoted, and so on... These are every day, all day, and everlasting, words that fit Jesus every time and any time!

"Jesus Christ the same yesterday, and today, and forever." **(Hebrews 13:8)**

100% Looks Like

One hundred percent looks like Jesus who leaves nothing out. We give him a prayer here and a prayer there hoping it will suffice. Well, it isn't enough. We ask, we want, and we need, but can't follow through after the blessings been given.

Jesus wants your whole heart. Not when it suits you. Not because you're in a good mood. Not because you think everything is alright. He is not a shelf time commodity; nor, should the Lord be used only when it is convenient.

One hundred percent on your part should look like consistency in relationship, fellowshipping with other believers, reading His daily word, and spreading the Gospel of Jesus Christ.

Accountability is one hundred percent!

***"I will praise thee with my whole heart..."* (Psalm 138:1)**

Distractions

Please note that distractions are tactful tools that the enemy uses to deter you from anything related to your relationship with the Lord Jesus Christ.

If the enemy can get you to focus on something else your peace can be misplaced; your hope can be discouraged; your mindset can be altered for his good.

Getting you off task is his vice. A simple argument can turn mountainous. Misery loves company. Be aware of the enemy at all times. He is aware of you at all times. You could be singing praises and the enemy will place your attention elsewhere. Be aware!

"The thief does not come except to steal, and to kill, and to destroy. I have come that they may have life, and that they may have it more abundantly." **(John 10:10)**

Yet Will I Trust Him

Yes, trials seem to dim your way, but on other grounds is sinking sand. Man's decisions can't be trusted day by day. Jesus remains the same yesterday, today, and forevermore. You may get weary and the route may appear to get bleary, but the road still remains.

Although you've done wrong and your thoughts have wandered off, his forgiveness is available. When the situation comes around again the conclusion has an alternate ending. You know His way is best because you've tried your own and ended up in a mess. Your rescue was a lesson. The circumstances you go through are not a curse but a blessing; so your trust in him should be never failing.

"Your word is a lamp to my feet And a light to my path." **(Psalm 119:105)**

Whole Healed Go

In the Bible Jesus healed Ten Lepers, Jesus sent them to show themselves to the priests. Only one came back to say, "Thank you." Being healed is a physical thing. Being made whole is a spiritual thing.

It's that relationship part. It's that extra part that includes wisdom concerning the Kingdom of the Lord.

Whole means all parts. The other nine lepers only received a part of their blessing. The whole can only be recognized by the Lord and like-minded folks. Being made whole comes with peace, joy, insight. And faith becomes operable, in a different sense, because of who Jesus is!

"And He said to him, "Arise, go your way. Your faith has made you well." (Luke 17:19)

Power and Authority

Operating in the power and authority God gives you is life-changing. You can have one and lack the other. The Lord has given us territories (power) to have dominion (authority) over. You have the power to control your home, but are you acting in the authority to do so?

You have the power to change your ways but are you using the authority it takes to do so. The spirit of God within you has given you the means to operate in both. As disciples of Christ, it is imperative that you maneuver in the power and the authority given you. Cast out demons, pray for those that ask for prayer, and speak healing over other's lives. Are you using power and authority?

"Then He called His twelve disciples together, and gave them power and authority over all devils, and to cure diseases." **(Luke 9:1)**

Baggage

When traveling by air your baggage has to be a certain weight. If it doesn't meet the requirements, you'll have to pay extra. Some remove things for to lighter baggage. Some people go ahead and pay the price for the extra weight.

Are you paying the price for too much weight? You can acquire more weight when ministering, because you give advice and want to check-up on the person/s without first consulting God. Before you know it their problem becomes yours. We also can obtain weight by worrying and not praying for others and their issues. Sometimes just telling someone to**,** *"Cast all your cares upon him…,"* **(1 Peter 5:7)** is a powerful resolve!

"And He said to them, *"Take nothing for the journey, neither staffs nor bag nor bread nor money; and do not have two tunics apiece"* **(Luke 9:3).**

The Oil

The oil of God is placed upon me to cover my infirmities. The oil of God blankets me to hide me from the vultures that seek to consume me. As my flesh dies daily, they're made aware of the carnal death falling off me. The oil of God is placed upon me to quench that certain thirst that my soul needs. It desires that river of life that Jesus has made available for me.

The oil of God has been braided with the tears from my face to acknowledge his mercy, favor, and grace. In time, since the oil is lighter it stays on top as a covering, sheltering my emotions with intentional healing. The oil of God that's placed upon me has saturated my heart to overthrow my will. The oil of God is placed upon me like a blessed hymn and I fall to my knees in gratefulness.

"The LORD is their strength, and He is the saving refuge of His anointed." **(Psalm 28:8)**

P.U.S.H.

"Pray Until Something Happens." "Until the door opens praise him in the hallway." These phrases are meant for you to endure, press on, keep the faith, and hang in there.

We are on God's time. Don't fret he's got your back. He is aware of your needs and problems. He knows of you personally. So, whether in sunshine or rain, continue to hold on. This is an encouraging message. If you are reading this right now, please note that God has not forgotten the things which concern you.

"The LORD will perfect that which concerns me; Your mercy, O LORD, endures forever; Do not forsake the works of Your hands." **(Psalm 138:8)**

Broken is Okay

Jesus didn't hang around those who thought they were perfect and had it together. He positioned himself with the poor, sick, downhearted, despondent, and people society regarded as useless.

He still welcomes the brokenhearted; the lonely, and troubled in mind. It's okay! Jesus can use those who are searching for that "because you first loved me" relationship."

He is faithful and He will put those broken pieces together again. He will polish you up and place his beacon of light in you. You don't have to wait until everything is alright in your life. NOW, is the appropriate time!

"But now, O LORD, You are our Father; We are the clay, and You our potter; And all we are the work of Your hand." **(Isaiah 64:8)**

It's For Him

If you keep in mind that whatsoever you do, do it as unto the Lord, then you won't look for validation or a "good job" response from others. If you greet people just so they will greet you back, you're greeting them for your own satisfaction. When they don't respond, anger, rolled eyes, or an attitude will cross your thoughts.

The Bible talks about loving one another. It also speaks about doing unto others' as you would have them do unto you. It doesn't say do what they do to you.

It's all for and unto Jesus. Is anything more important than the Lord?

"He who does not love does not know God, for God is love." (1 John 4:8) "And whatever you do in word or deed, do all in the name of the Lord Jesus, giving thanks to God the Father through Him." **(Colossians 3:17)**

Rejection

Being rejected is not a good feeling. Not getting that seemingly perfect job or loving someone who doesn't display the same emotions can hurt. When you put your life in the hands of Jesus Christ please note that He knows what's best. Consider it a spiritual release. Rejection means it was not intended for you.

You may not ever understand why things didn't work out. Be reassured that, the Lord knows best. He is perfect in all his ways. Our decisions can be emotionally based, financially rushed, and just wrong. The Lord accepts Society's rejects. Jesus was rejected by his own. So, he understands. Let your faith embrace his will.

: "The stone which the builders rejected Has become the chief cornerstone." **(Mark 12:10)**

The Yoke

A yoke is known as a harness. It constrains the wearer from freely moving about. Sometimes it feels as if this flesh we're constrained in a slaving sin pit. There are so many opportunities in the world to help you make wrong decisions, come to judgmental conclusions, and end up with emotional outcomes. Yet, the yoke of sin can be broken if you understand the difference between being in this world and being of it.

Being in this world, you are subjected to the ups and downs, ins and outs, and forward and backward. Being not of this world you understand God's choice above the world's standards and options. Jesus will always have a better option, way-out, or outcome. The bonds of sin can be broken forever! The reward is out of this world!

"Stand fast therefore in the liberty by which Christ has made us free, and do not be entangled again with a yoke of bondage." **(Galatians 5:1)**

Freedom With Liberty

When the slaves were freed, there were not given liberty. Freedom means having the power or right to think, act, or speak without hindrance. Liberty, on the other hand, is the state of being free without oppression from authorities concerning one's life or behaviors. In other words, the slaves were free from slavery, but could not walk through the front door of certain establishments. So, their liberty was restrained.

In Christ Liberty and Freedom come together. The veil was rent at Calvary. That means you can go to God without permission or restriction. Feel free to praise God anytime. Guess what? Victory comes with your Praises. Feel free to ask and bask in receiving from God. Feel the liberty of walking in the will of God with a smile. The happiness, gratefulness, and security that comes from this liberty are joyous feelings!

"For in him we live, and move, and have our being." **(Act 17:28)**

Anyhow

Complaining serves no purpose. You are just running your mouth unnecessarily. While you are complaining, you speak life or death to someone?

Can you change what you are complaining about? If so, why aren't you making the change? Are you a part of the problem? If it is past your means then prayer must intervene.

Trust Jesus anyhow. Be grateful anyhow. When people are just being people, praise the Lord anyhow.

Praise breaks yokes. Praise brings a joyful noise. Praise will lift burdens. Praise! Praise! Praise!

Pray, accept, release, and move forward. Move forward in your "Anyhow" mindset!

"Do all things without murmurings and disputings." (Philippians 2:14)

Know Who's On Your Ship

Who's on your ship, meaning whose got your back? Who's on your team? Are your friends the "yes" crew agreeing to every decision you make? Is there any chance of mutiny? Do they understand your goals and purpose? Do you?

Sometimes you can't get where you're supposed to, because of those around you. Some relationships aren't meant to last. On your ship or support group each crew member has their position. His presence on the ship caused confusion. He wasn't supposed to be on the ship.

"But Jonah arose to flee to Tarshish from the presence of the Lord." **(Jonah 1:3)**

S. E. R. V. E.

Have we forgotten that we are servants of Christ? Do you know what it means to serve? In Christ, your title means nothing, if being a servant of Christ is not your mindset.

S-acrafice and surrender your will for His.
E-dify, equip, empower, encourage, & empathy.
   Incorporate these words every day.
Re-build, restore, refurbish, reiterate, and
   righteousness. These are reoccurrences.
V-ocalize the victory of God's visions and values.
E-mpty yourself of everything earthly.

"... not with eyeservice, as men-pleasers, but as bond-servants of Christ, doing the will of God from the heart." **(Ephesians 6:6)**

I'm A Prisoner

Did you know you can be snatched out of the clutches of sin and death? When you think of Salvation that way, you appreciate the cuffs of mercy that will prevent you from things you thought you should have or hold. This ball and chain of mercy will keep you girded up for survival at a certain pace. Those bars of favor allow you to reach out to man. But man cannot harm you, because of the boundaries of the bars. There's always an eye on you.

The comparison to a prison extends to being captured. When you are in prison, all of your provisions are provided. This comes with an abundant harvest. Yes, there are boundaries. but stay on the grounds of righteousness. It's internal freedom. You will be rescued from yourself for yourself.

"For this cause I Paul, the prisoner of Jesus Christ for you Gentiles..." **(Ephesians 3:1)**

Fearful Or Faithful

You cannot live these words at the same time and be effective. Living in fear can bring on other spirits, mental dysfunctions, and bad habits. Fear will inhibit your lifestyle, relationships, and esteem.

Walking by faith constitutes a different walk. It can extinguish anxiousness and blot out worry. Being faithful is a discipline. Faithful runs along with trust. Jesus is faithful in our lives, whether you know or not.

Fearing things that you can't change and have no control over will cause you to react on desperate terms. You're faithful in putting clothes on your physical man. Why not invest in trying on Jesus for your spiritual man? It will fit!

"For God has not given us a spirit of fear, but of power and of love and of a sound mind." **(2 Timothy 1:7)**

Last To First

Being last in line can boggle the nerves. Having a last name beginning with the last letter of the alphabet can bother you. Being the baby or last child can be bothersome also. You're always last. I have good news.

Jesus is drawn towards those that society has deemed last, lost, and not important. If you feel unimportant to the world, so what, this world is fickle. One day you're at the top. When you make a mistake; someone comes along who is better (in their eyes); people get bored with you; you've become old news. Then you're at the bottom again.

Jesus loves you. You are always important to him; you are so important. I'm encouraging you to go on. You can make it.

"So the last will be first, and the first last. For many are called, but few chosen." **(Mathew 20:16)**

More Than You Can

People will often say that "The Lord will not give you more than you can bear." More needs to be said. Physically you may think that you can't take anymore. You may be on the verge of giving up hope. You may be on the boundaries of life. You may be so weakened that your knees start to buckle and "Faint not" is not what your intentions are.

Spiritually you're being held up by grace. Halleluiah! Well, it's okay to fall, but make sure you're falling back into the arms of Jesus. Falling into apprehension is not the Lord's intention. He wills that you depend fully on Him. Knowing that makes you worry-free. Depending on the Lord daily is a good walk.

"The steps of a good man are ordered by the LORD, And He delights in his way." **(Psalm 37:23)**

Through

Through is the process of continuing in time out to the other side. There are places in the Bible where the Lord put someone through the desert, or the valley, or some other distress. Knowing that there is an exit in what you are going through should place you in praise mode. Say to yourself, "the Lord will get the glory out of this situation."

Your through is a learning tool. Your through is an investment for the kingdom of God. Your through should provide proof to someone else that Jesus can bring you out.

Your through should end with a praise at His feet. Your through should increase your faith and decrease yourself. Your through should encourage you to move forward. There is always an exit at the end of your through!

"Weeping may endure for a night, but joy comes in the morning." **(Psalm 30:5)**

Disabled

Lord, disable this earthly walk of mine and create in me a righteous stride to walk on the path purposed for me. Lord, incapacitate these arms and hands that reach out to entertain man. Form them into instruments of praises that are dedicated to you. Jesus, deactivate this one-track mind that has borders and boundaries.

Install that unwavering faith and trust in you that exceeds past these earthly matters. My Savior, immobilize this polluted heart and filter it to beat to the rhythms of love. Resuscitate my wants with the purities of your will. Incline my sight. Deliverer, mold me into what you'll have me to be. This Servant is only designed for you.

***"Show me Your ways, O LORD; Teach me Your paths."* (Psalm 25:4)**

Called and Chosen

When called upon from the Lord, sometimes we are not in that place to hear him. We have placed so many things in front of him without knowing it. Our cell phones are always in a place where we can hear that ringtone. What in your life is blocking you from hearing that call from Jesus?

When chosen, running from that call seems useless. You will always end up coming back to Jesus. Those worldly goals that you made won't feel the same. Everything you do will feel uncomfortable, because of the spiritual calling on your life.

Stop wasting time and adhere to the word of God. He and others are waiting. That thirsting inside of you for relief can only be quenched by responding to the call the "Living God."

"The LORD is near to all who call upon Him, To all who call upon Him in truth." **(Psalm 143:18)**

Addiction/Deliverance

There are numerous things that you can be addicted to. You can be addicted to ritual. Worldly possessions can be addicting (cars, money, clothes, food, technology, sex, social media, etc.…). People can be addicted to people. (Celebrities' friends, family, etc.…). Change is uncomfortable for lots of people. Don't let the world label you with addictions. Declare deliverance and don't adapt to the word "addiction!" **"…And I kept myself from my iniquity." (Psalm 18:48)**

There's a Deliverer who can change your life upon a request. You have to know the need for change. How can you face what you don't realize? Don't let what's on this earth keep you on this earth. Deliverance is freedom. If you need a meeting, go but watch what you call yourself!

"For as he thinketh in his heart, so is he…" **(Proverbs 23:7)**

Intensify

Some words that are associated with the word intensify are: boost, raise, increase, magnify, reinforce, deepen, and heighten. Jesus doesn't want mediocre praise. He is not an ordinary God. He sits high and, at the same time, meets you where you are.

Our sovereign God deserves an intensified praise; heightened worship designed to tell of his greatness. You do your best at work to get that bonus and raise. Jesus is worthy of your exceptional praise and your undivided attention. Why would I give him conventional praise? Magnify your time with Jesus. He is worthy of an intensified you.

***"Through the LORD's mercies we are not consumed, Because His compassions fail not."* (Lamentations 3:22-23)**

The Others

The others won't understand the plans the Lord has set for you. The others will go on day to day discounting the Lord's place in you. The others aren't designed to do what's predestined in you.

The others' ears are not inclined to hear, nor can they dictate what is only for you. The others dwell in the darkness, bumping into obstacles. They are content with carnal vision and in denial concerning their spiritual receptacles.

Others seek rewards that last for a moment. So Jesus says, I have provided you with a testimony to introduce them to me "The Living Water."

"But Jesus said to him, "Follow Me, and let the dead bury their own dead." **(Matthew 8:22)**

Man

Man substitutes, makes excuses, and dwells in conditions. Man operates without integrity while distracted by ambitions. Man is happy, sad, and lonely; too emotional. Man has to progress in stages and his agenda is mostly personal.

Man searches for satisfaction in common places. Man conquers the weak with smiling faces. Man's endurance must be greeted with a prize. Man seeks earthly riches with words laced in lies.

Man indulges in wayward living. Man obtains selfish spoils while conveniently giving. Be aware of an open hand that lowers as you grab hold of it. Be prayerful of man for they do not understand why they do it.

"I find then a law, that evil is present with me, the one who wills to do good." **(Romans 7:21)**

God

God has no limits, no boundaries, and no borders. God is consistent and operates in order. God is great and owns the cattle on a thousand hills. The Lord dwells in praise; he sits in the midst of them.

God gave his son Jesus to be an ultimate sacrifice. Jesus was the sacrificial lamb to redeem man's life.

Jesus requires us to love thy neighbor and come out of the night. Vessel of honor, Jesus has chosen you to spread the Gospel of Jesus Christ.

"Come out from among them And be separate, says the Lord. Do not touch what is unclean, And I will receive you." **(2 Corinthians 6:17)**

Rise Above To Win

The world's emotional chaos can bring you down. Rise above the confusion and let love abound. Rise above the bitterness; surge pass the hate. Climb past depression and the need to retaliate.

Soar above judgment, envy is shaken off. Surpass being anxious, while your emptiness is filled with love. Spin around false intentions and feel your faith mature and grow. Let your faith excel above your enemies into atmospheres of joy.

Let your self-esteem and self-worth embrace each other as long-time parted friends Then, as you greet them with confidence, you will blossom in victory. Let your smile override the tears of bounded wants. Ascend in freedom and liberty and let them entertain your weary thoughts. Remember to rise above.

"...we shall reap if we faint not." **(Galatians 6:9)**

The Lord Changeth Not

In this world changes are common. Change will not always recognize time or space. Change may happen whether you are ready or not. Change does not take time to disagree or contemplate. Locations change. There are atmospheric changes and geological changes.

People change, minds change, and temperaments change. Rules and laws change. Expect change to interfere with your plans. Accept that you will change. Everything changes, but the Lord. He will do what his word says!

"For I am the LORD, I change not." **(Malachi 3:6)**

Why

Why seek what the Lord speaks? Why stare upon the things you keep? Why dwell on the unchangeable? Why reach for the unattainable? Why respond to the unresponsive? Why attempt to move what you think is rooted? Why complain about the judgments? Why perform in darkness? Why call out to the deaf? Why claim what another has left?

Why summon the careless to hold the precious? Why face forward to turn around and listen? Why stand backward on the frontline? Why not turn a deaf ear, to mankind? Why remember those forgotten? Why not expose what you are pocketing? Why? Because of FAITH! Believe what the world deems impossible. Don't walk through a wall when you know the doorkeeper?

"... if you have faith as a mustard seed, you will say to this mountain, 'Move from here to there,' and it will move;" **(Matthew 17:20)**

Search Me

The eyes of God are upon me. Lord as you have glared in my soul and heart forgive me for my wrongs. In your hands is where I belong. I stand acknowledging you as King over my life. You are the shelter during my nights.

Your grace is sufficient.
Your mercy is expedient.
Careful are your strategies for me.
Blessed are the gifts, you bestow upon me.
Faithful are your intentions towards me.
Consistent are the victories surrounding me.

"O LORD, You have searched me and known me." **(Psalm 139:1).**

It's In Your Hands

Jesus has given us charge over territories. He has given us the power to handle what comes with this charge. He has given us the knowledge to keep this charge. He has given us the wisdom to operate in it.

Jesus has deposited in our hearts the procedures and tools to reconstruct the situations torn down. He has given us the thought process to fix and restore broken circumstances. He has *replaced* the condemning parts of our lives with a new foundation.

Take a seat disorder! Walk away fear! Don't even come near me confusion! Stop pulling on the door of doubt. Impatience has been swept away. Bravery has stepped forward.

"Arise, for the LORD has delivered the camp of Midian into your hand." **(Judges 7:15)**

I Receive It

The world deems you low. Jesus sees you high. The world said you couldn't have it. Jesus said to occupy.

Your friends see you lacking. Jesus says your cup is running over. Loved ones didn't believe you. Jesus is your covering.

The world won't let go of your past. Jesus saw your freedom before your past. The world sees you full of mess. Jesus has emptied your vessel and filled it with deliverance.

"And out of them all the Lord delivered me." **(Timothy 3:11)**

Give

Give in confidence and faith. Give in sickness and health. Give not to receive, but in responsibility. Give out of necessity. Give in obedience and sincerity. Give in love and in relationship. Give in servitude, reverence, and promise.

Give according to His riches and not yours. Give intentionally and not emotionally. Give in season and when the season is out. Give and reap the benefits while the world suffers drought.

"... for God loves a cheerful giver." **(2 Corinthians 9:7)**

Fall Back

Your raggedy righteousness is dressed in dirt. Yet, the Lord still hears your call when life starts to hurt. Your sinful conceptions have pushed your flesh forward. Allow the Lord to possess your reins so your flesh will fall backward.

"For thou hast possessed my reins." **(Psalm 139:13)**

For Bookings
Email: system.mwb@gmail.com
Website: www.miriamwbrice

www.ingramcontent.com/pod-product-compliance
Lightning Source LLC
Chambersburg PA
CBHW052121110526
44592CB00013B/1699